This Book is for:

_____

from:

_____

BRUISER THE BULLY

By

Yolanda Rambert

Illustrated by

Thaddeus Lavalais

Bruiser the Bully
By Yolanda Rambert

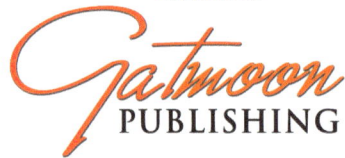

Publisher:

Gatmoon
PUBLISHING

Gatmoon Publishing, L.L.C.
P.O. Box 1244
Concord, North Carolina 28026
United States of America

Illustrations created by: Thaddeus Lavalais

Rambert, Yolanda
Bruiser the Bully
ISBN-13: 978-0692390733
ISBN-10: 0692390731
Library of Congress Cataloging-in-Publication Data

Bruiser was king of the playground and he ruled everyone around him. He had bright orange hair and freckles and was taller than all of the kids in his class.

"I'm Bruiser, king of the playground and I rule anyone who is around" he shouted.

2

Bruiser let out a
big laugh as he
marched to the
other end of
the playground.
He ripped the
        dinosaur
          right out
          of Paxx's hand.
          Matthew began to cry as
          Bruiser shouted "I'm king
          of the playground and I rule
        anyone who is around!"

Later on that night Paxx asked his mom if he could stay home from school. Paxx was frightened about what would happen the next day.

"Is everything ok?" his mom asked. "Are you feeling sick?" "No." Paxx replied. Paxx's mom looked at him curiously and asked "So why do you want to stay home?" "Well it's just, it's just and his voice trailed off with a small sigh. "Just what?" His mom replied. Paxx was thinking to himself 'oh boy, what do I tell mom?' Paxx couldn't think of what to say to his mother about the way he felt in school, so he decided to say, "Oh Mom, nothing, nothing at all, I will go to school tomorrow." Paxx's mom thought to herself there is something wrong he doesn't seem like himself lately but she just looked at her son lovingly and hugged him. She was going to get to the bottom of what was going on.

The next day at school during clean up after art class, Paxx walked over to his teacher, Mrs. Marshall, and just hung around not saying anything. Mrs. Marshall liked Paxx. He was a good student with excellent manners. He always tried his best every day and was helpful to her.

Mrs. Marshall looked at Paxx just standing there and she wondered what was on his mind, and before she could ask, Paxx blurted out "Can I stay in during recess, please, please?" "Why, Paxx, it's the only free time you will have to play. Why on Earth would you ever want to stay inside? Is everything ok?" Mrs. Marshall asked looking intently at Paxx. "Do you feel ill?" "No" replied Paxx, "it's just, it's just" sighing once more Paxx trailed off again. "Just what?" Mrs. Marshall asked as she looked over her eyeglasses. Paxx knew that when Mrs. Marshall looked over her eyeglasses she was on to the truth! So, Paxx quickly said "Nothing!" and quickly said "I will go to recess." Mrs. Marshall could see something was wrong, however, once again Paxx insisted everything was fine.

Bruiser the Bully ruled the playground for months and months without anyone saying a word. That is until one day a new student arrived. Anchor and his family were new to town. He had no idea about Bruiser the Bully during his first day at All Hope Elementary School.

That day during recess as usual, Bruiser yelled, "I'm king of the playground and I rule anyone who is around!"

All the kids began to tremble with fear. Even Paxx started to cry. Anchor asked him, "What is the matter?" Paxx said in a shaky voice, "That's Bruiser the Bully, and he is king of the playground. He rules anyone who is around and that includes you!"

11

All at once Anchor marched right up to Bruiser and shouted "What you are doing is bullying and that is not right!"

All of the kids gathered around peering at Anchor in awe. Anchor was much smaller than Bruiser and here he was standing up to Bruiser the Bully!

Everyone else was so afraid of Bruiser but not Anchor. The students at All Hope Elementary School would have never dared to confront Bruiser about his bad behavior.

13

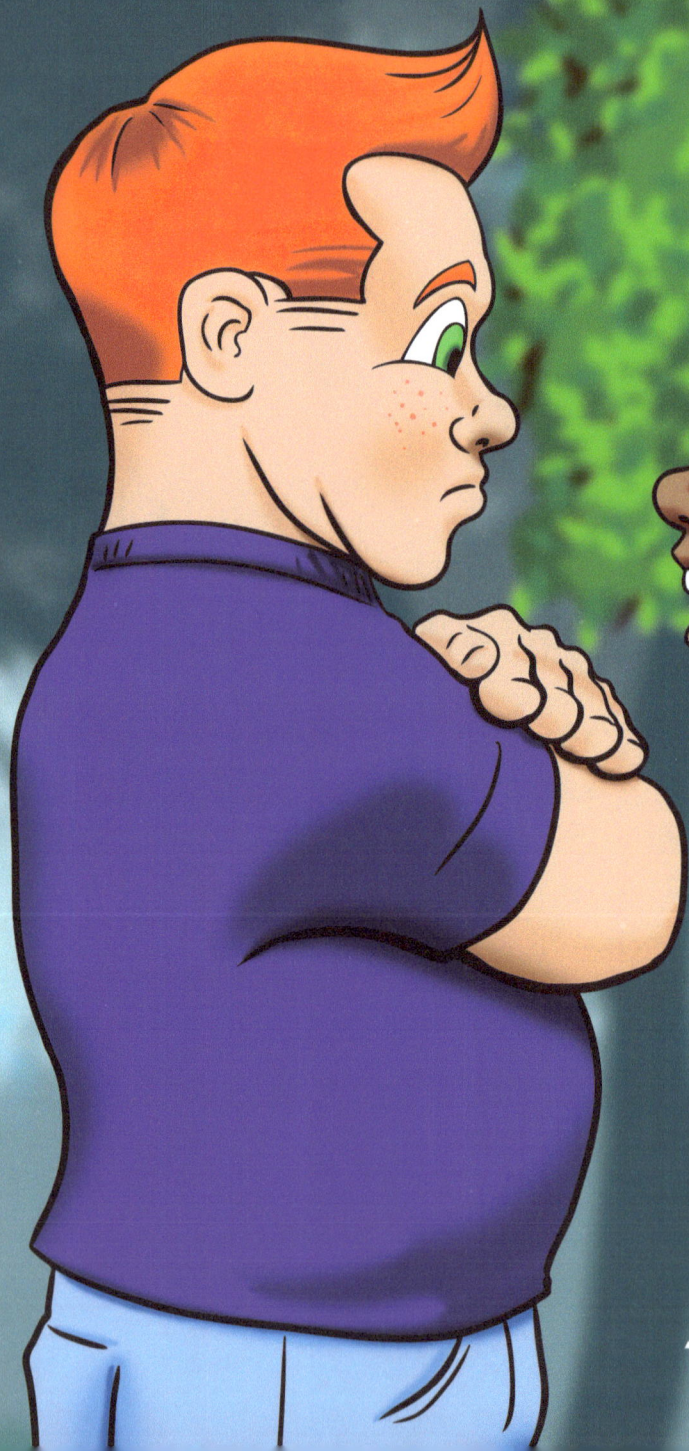

Anchor went on saying to Bruiser "In my old school a Counselor came to speak to my class about bullying, and said anytime you or someone is being bullied you should tell an adult and never be afraid to tell when someone is bothering you." Bruiser was nervous. He didn't want to get into trouble with his teacher or better yet the Principal. Anchor asked Bruiser "Why would you want to hurt your friends?" Bruiser answered "They are not my friends. In my old school the kids always made fun of me because I was taller than everyone else and because I had freckles. They didn't want to be my friend because they said I looked like a giant and I didn't belong there. I wasn't going to give anyone here a chance to make fun of me so I decided to become a bully to protect myself."

16

"So you mean to tell me you've never even given them a chance to be your friends?" asked Anchor. "Why should I?" replied Bruiser. "They will just make fun of me." "I would love to be your friend" said Anchor excitedly. "I think being tall is so cool and I hope to be as tall as you one day." "You do?" then Bruiser scratched his head and said "Wow!"

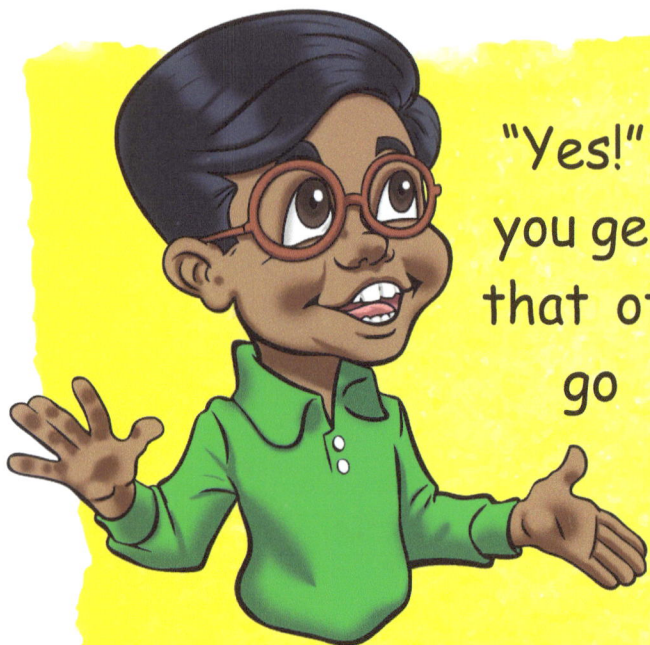

"Yes!" shouted Anchor. "Bruiser, you get to do a lot of cool things that other kids can't. You can go on all the rides at the amusement park that most of us are too short to get on, and you're always the first one to get picked for sports like basketball. That's because everyone always wants the tallest person on their team." "Well I never thought about it that way. Maybe you're right," said Bruiser, smiling for the first time EVER!

18

Bruiser apologized to Paxx and all the kids on the playground for the way he had treated them. Everyone was happy that they didn't have to be fearful during recess any more. "Would you like to play tag?" Anchor asked. "Boy would I. That's one of my favorite games!" shouted Bruiser.

Anchor smiled. He was glad he could help. From that day on Bruiser said goodbye to bullying.

THE END

GET HELP NOW!

Bullying can affect you in many ways. You may lose sleep or feel sick. You may want to skip school. You may even be thinking about suicide. If you are feeling hopeless or helpless or know someone that is, please call the **LIFELINE** at **1-800-273-TALK (8255)**.

The Roles Kids Play

There are many roles that kids can play. Kids can bully others, they can be bullied, or they may witness bullying. When kids are involved in bullying, they often play more than one role. Sometimes kids may both be bullied and bully others or they may witness other kids being bullied. It is important to understand the multiple roles kids play in order to effectively prevent and respond to bullying.

Importance of Not Labeling Kids

When referring to a bullying situation, it is easy to call the kids who bully others "bullies" and those who are targeted "victims," but this may have unintended consequences. When children are labeled as "bullies" or "victims" it may:

- Send the message that the child's behavior cannot change
- Fail to recognize the multiple roles children might play in different bullying situations
- Disregard other factors contributing to the behavior such as peer influence or school climate

Instead of labeling the children involved, focus on the behavior. For instance:

- Instead of calling a child a "bully," refer to them as "the child who bullied"
- Instead of calling a child a "victim," refer to them as "the child who was bullied"
- Instead of calling a child a "bully/victim," refer to them as "the child who was both bullied and bullied others."

Kids Involved in Bullying

The roles kids play in bullying are not limited to those who bully others and those who are bullied. Some researchers talk about the "circle of bullying" to define both those directly involved in bullying and those who actively or passively assist the behavior or defend against it. Direct roles include:

- **Kids who Bully:** These children engage in bullying behavior towards their peers. There are many risk factors that may contribute to the child's involvement in the behavior. Often, these students require support to change their behavior and address any other

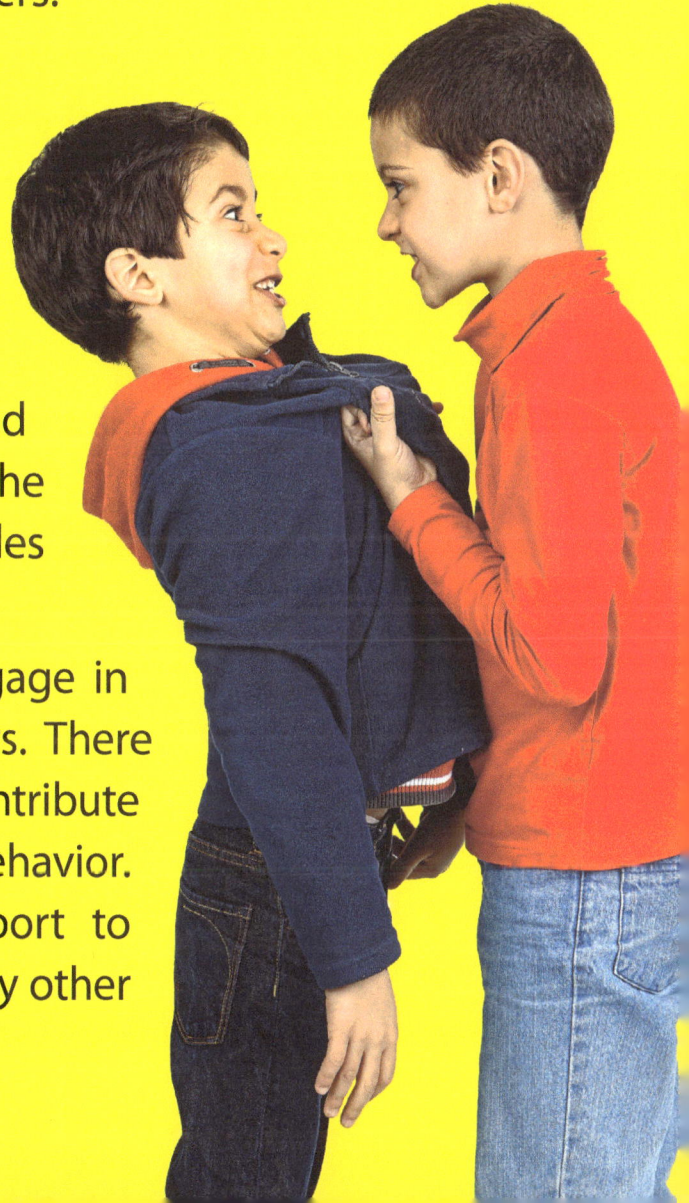

challenges that may be influencing their behavior.

- **Kids who are Bullied:** These children are the targets of bullying behavior. Some factors put children at more risk of being bullied, but not all children with these characteristics will be bullied. Sometimes, these children may need help learning how to respond to bullying.

- Even if a child is not directly involved in bullying, they may be contributing to the behavior. Witnessing the behavior may also affect the child, so it is important for them to learn what they should do when they see bullying happen. Roles kids play when they witness bullying include:

- **Kids who Assist:** These children may not start the bullying or lead in the bullying behavior, but serve as an "assistant" to children who are bullying. These children may encourage the bullying behavior and occasionally join in.

Notes

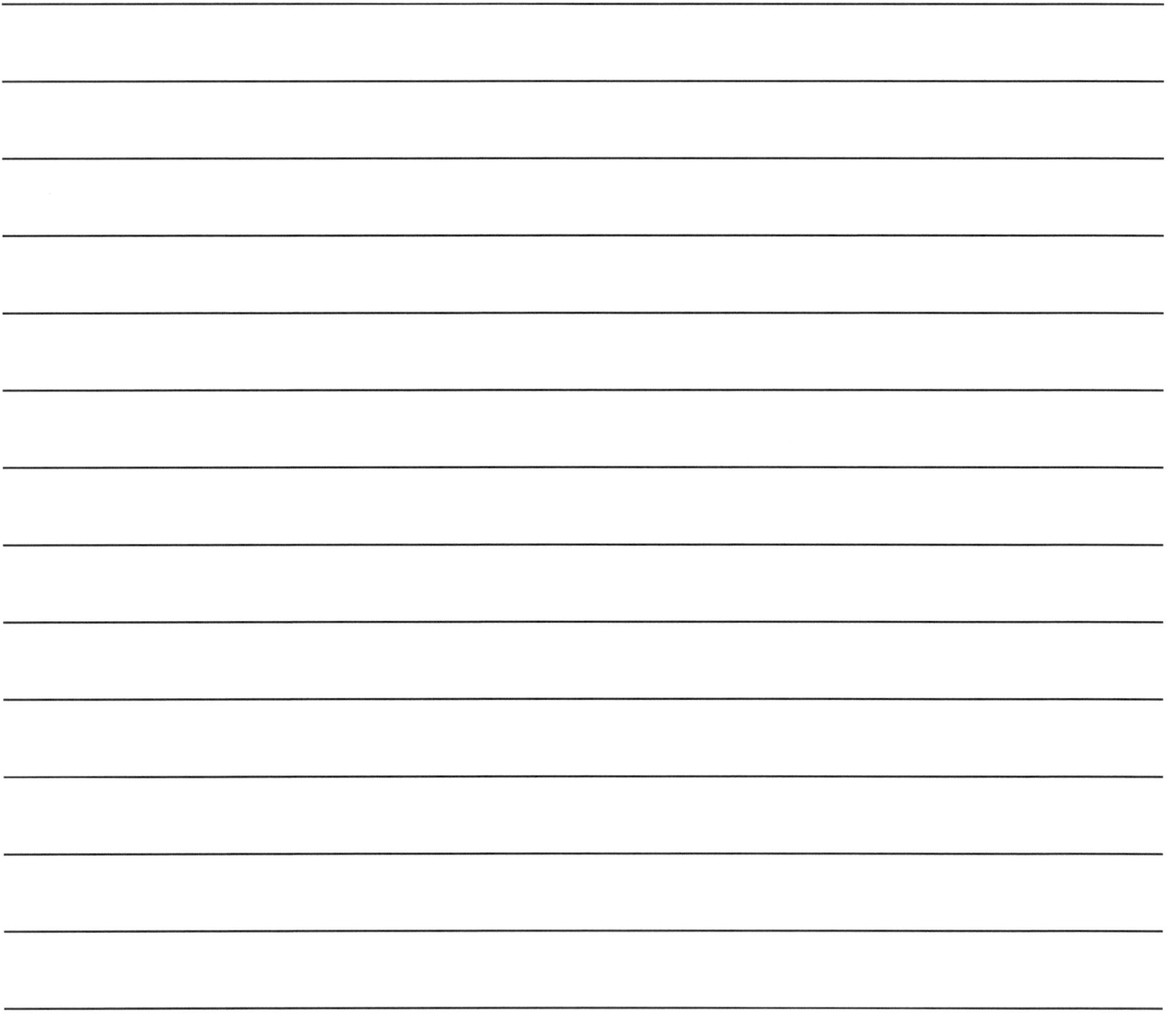